Her Undisclosed Desires

J. Sexton

Foreword

We all have our own concept of the perfect love. Some of us are lucky enough to find it. Others can merely dream, and hope that, one day, it will find them.

The poetry in this book reflects a yearning for a passionate, committed, honest, sensual, caring, all-encompassing, and dedicated type of love, one that accepts flaws and imperfections, and never turns its back. It is about desires that may never be expressed, but are always there, waiting for the right one to share them with.

We all have our hidden desires, and maybe one day, we can realise them.

Jo Sexton, October 2021

Her Undisclosed Desires

Him

My Love

I watch him, marvelling at the way he moves, like a tiger, proud and almost predatory. I crave him like nobody before, in every single way, yet in that moment, I hold back, watching him from beneath my lashes.

He cannot see the desire in my eyes, but he knows that it is there. He knows beyond a shadow of a doubt how I feel, for it is reflected in his heart. Yet, he asks me to hold back, to keep him guessing, to hide it until we are alone. It is our little game, and, although it is difficult, I will do it for him.

And so, I sit, my legs crossed demurely at the ankles, my hands folded in my lap, straightening my back very slightly to savour the feel of my silk blouse on my painfully erect nipples.

I want him, badly, and have been waiting for his arrival all day. He knows; I know he knows, and he makes me wait nevertheless. He likes to have me wet and wanton, desperate for his touch. And I love to please him, as he pleases me.

I will wait, patiently, yet in a heightened state of arousal. I know that it - that *he* - will be worth it.

Deep in the realm

of my fantasies,

you and I

exist together

in a permanent tangle

of limbs,

of hearts,

and of souls.

Your eyes compel me,

your words

captivate me,

your body

attracts me,

yet your heart

is the seal

that keeps me glued

to your side.

His lips have

an allure

all of their own

and she can

lose herself

for hours

in the poetry

of his kiss.

There is nothing

more addictive than

the way he

showed me

again and again

that he was exactly

who he said

he was.

It was as if he had stepped straight out of her dreams and into her arms. He was everything she had imagined and hoped for; strong yet gentle, dominant yet caring. She was overcome with desire, not just to feel him inside her, but also to feel his soul rest comfortably against hers.

His smile is crooked

and his eyes

are black as sin,

and I want

nothing more than

to immerse myself

in his own brand

of delicious inferno.

She waits for him

with bated breath,

anticipation and desire

burning inside;

he is all she wants

and all she needs,

and the fire of her passion

will smoulder

long after he is by her side.

He sees me. He looks beyond the body and the face and the lips, and he sees the real me. Right into the heart of me, along with all of my scars and my flaws and my imperfections. And despite them all, he stays, and he loves me anyway.

His love

is the match

that sets me alight,

and his passion

keeps me burning

throughout the night.

I could lose myself

in your eyes

as I melt

under your gaze,

crying out for you

in my most secret

of places,

craving you

deep inside.

Your name

trips off my tongue

like honeyed elixir;

breathlessly uttered,

dripping with desire,

on the cusp of

ecstasy.

There was something different about him. Something she hasn't encountered before. It was in the way he made her feel so safe, yet ignited a fire in her veins. In the way he calmed all of her fears and patiently coaxed down her walls. But more than anything, it was in the way he saw straight through her, saw all of her flaws, yet accepted and loved her anyway.

It is strange

yet beautiful,

the way you dominate

my thoughts

as thoroughly as

you dominate

my body.

I crave your body,

I crave your depth,

I crave the feel of you

as you fill me

so completely,

spurred on by

such exquisite desire;

I crave your lips

against mine, your body

pressing me into

these sheets,

claiming me,

possessing me,

for I am yours

as you are mine.

You don't have to

be gentle with my body

as long as

you are gentle

with my heart;

I can withstand

rough, passionate intensity

if I never have cause

to doubt your love.

Take me,

wrap me up in

the silken threads

of your possession;

make me yours

in every way possible ~

I will come for you,

I will scream for you

in all the right places.

There is a wildness in me that only he can contain, a wildness that I reserve only for him. He doesn't attempt to belittle me, or shame me for my passions. Instead, he runs with me, he coaxes me, he urges me to be the best that I can be – for myself as well as for him.

He whispers into her ear,

"you're mine,"

and she swoons,

her knees weak with

unadulterated passion,

for nothing

turns her on more

than commitment,

loyalty, and dominant desire.

He reads me

so thoroughly,

unfolding me carefully

for his inspection,

lapping his tongue

around my words,

absorbing the meaning

held within,

perceiving the things

I do not say,

so sensitive to

my needs;

he understands me

completely.

His love was like nothing she had ever experienced before. Full of passion, and intensity, and fun, and friendship. And desire; oh, the desire! It was everything she had ever dreamt of. He was everything she would ever need.

She thinks of you

in the darkness

of the night,

imagining

how you'd feel,

tracing the memory

of you on

her heated skin;

She thinks of you

in the daylight,

wondering

how you are,

where you are,

and when she will

see you next –

she thinks of you

all the time.

He awakens

a passion in me

that rivals

no other;

I am his

for the taking,

heart, body,

and soul.

He took me by surprise, turning up the way that he did. Love had jaded me and I wasn't even sure that type of happiness could exist, at least for people like me. But he came along, and he was just *him*, so much him, and he blew me away. Yes, he swept me off my feet. He made me feel special, and important, and desired. I found myself craving his presence and missing him when he wasn't there. And that is when I knew. This was what people spoke about with such reverence. This was real love.

You watch my lips

intently

as I speak,

and I know that

you are dying

to kiss me;

I watch you

watching me

and I melt inside

at the desire

in your eyes

~

please,

ravage me now,

for I crave you immensely.

Your fingertips

trail a blaze

of feeling

down my bare arm,

setting my senses

on fire,

until I could almost

ignite with need

for you;

come closer

and let me

show you

exactly what you

do to me.

You whisper

to my soul

and I awaken inside,

blossoming

under your touch;

my body hungers for you,

my mind craves you,

and my heart envelops you,

inviting you inside.

Everything about him makes my life so much richer. The way he treats me like his princess yet handles me so firmly. The way he supports every aspect of my life, yet knows when to challenge me. The way he touches my face when he kisses me and tangles his hands in my hair. The way he loves me so completely, every part of me.

It felt like dying,

the way

you brought me

to the brink

and then

caught me as I fell;

I will always trust you

to love me

completely.

Like a hothouse flower

craves the rain –

intensely,

and often –

immerse me

in the river of

your passion

and watch me

bloom.

Bind me

and captivate me

with the strength of

your desire;

entwine me

in your passion –

I am a slave

to your love.

Your words

play havoc with

my mind

and my body,

sending waves

of pleasure

down my spine

that pool in

dark, swirling

deliciousness

between my thighs;

you set me alight,

you melt my inhibitions,

you drive me insane

with want,

with intense need –

take me,

I am yours.

And the best thing about him? He lifts me up. He makes me feel amazing about myself, and he does it without expecting anything in return. His heart is big and his love is pure and my happiness is top of his agenda, and this makes me love him all the more.

He worships me,

firm yet gentle hands

on sensitive skin,

tracing my

curves and contours

with reverence,

exalting in my

warm and wet depths

and the way I

sheath him so

tightly and

protectively;

he savours my taste

and always

comes back for more.

He touches me

in ways that

I can't explain

but which

resonate with me

on a deeper level –

deeper than mere skin

and bodily pleasure;

he touches my very soul.

His love is fierce

passionate,

and all-encompassing,

and she craves

the way he

desires her

so completely;

the way he

grabs her hair

in possessive fists,

pulling her taut,

opening her wide,

laying her bare

before him,

so he can love her right.

There is a fire in me

that burns

for you alone

with unswerving

and aching passion;

I crave your body

over me and

your thoughts

inside of me,

seeing me, knowing me,

without us having

to speak a word.

He was a gentleman

in all the right places,

until we were

behind closed doors,

and then he was

most deliciously not.

It was in the gentle touch of his hand as he brushed her hair from her face. It was in the way he handled her insecurities with such patience and understanding. It was in the way he looked at her and took in every part of her, even the bits she tried to hide. It was in the way he smiled at her and made her believe in the possibility of forever. It was in the way that he showed her this was love.

I think I am obsessed

with the way he

handles me,

kissing the scars

that he can't see

as gently as he

caresses the ones

that he can.

His hands,

oh, his hands;

they excite me

beyond compare,

playing my body

like no other,

teasing and coaxing me

to unknown realms

of pleasure,

yet at the same time,

soothing me

and calming my soul –

I am proud

to be his.

He understands me

in ways that nobody else

has done before;

I know that

I can trust him with

my everything

as he shows me

his love in so many

different ways.

He is the

pulse that is beating

through my veins;

he is the desire

that keeps

my body aflame.

He is my morning,

my afternoon,

and all through

my night,

and I couldn't

live without him

even if I tried.

He writes poetry

on my skin

with every touch

of his hand

and builds castles

in my heart

with the strength

of his love.

He amazes me

with the way

he instinctively knows

exactly what I need,

may it be a loving gesture,

a kind word,

or his hands,

tightly gripping my hair,

as he takes me roughly.

Maybe he isn't

my soulmate;

maybe we are just two people

who were drawn together,

our hearts singing

an identical song,

of love and mutual desire

and respect, and that's why

it works so well.

I never knew

what it

truly meant

to hunger for

someone

until I met you.

He tastes of

coffee and incense

and the darkest

of sin,

smooth yet gently spiced

on my tongue,

overwhelming

my senses

with his delicious flavour.

Spell my name

in the shape of

your kisses

over my hot,

tormented skin;

you don't need words

to tell me

exactly what

you want.

He is my strength,

there for me

when I need him

the most,

and he is

my weakness,

breaking down

my defences

with his love.

I come undone

under your

scorching gaze

as you undress me with

your eyes,

your hands tantalisingly close,

sending shivers

of pure desire

running through my veins.

Your hands

have the strength to

hold me together

when I

come undone;

to pull me back

and then

take me to the edge

again and again.

I dream of you

in tantalising

technicolour,

arousing my

senses

until I squirm

with desire;

I can feel

your hands

on my skin

and your lips against mine

and it is driving

me wild with

unresolved passion –

I need you here.

Let me show you

what you have

done to me,

turning me to jelly,

melting me

inside,

making me

swoon for you.

Words fail me

when you run

your hands

over my curves,

your lips

soft against my skin,

setting me alight,

making me

gasp and melt

simultaneously.

I begged you

for salvation

but you continued,

bringing me

to the cusp of bliss,

time and time again,

only to pull

me back,

edging me

so completely,

making me wild and weak

with desire.

He delivers his kisses

like love letters

onto my skin,

open-mouthed,

raw and vulnerable

in his want,

waiting in

breathless anticipation

for my reply.

I want your sins

and your secrets,

your fantasies and

your deepest dreams

and desires;

drown me in

your hunger,

capture me with

your passion,

consume me

and make me

yours.

His words

are hypnotic,

infusing my mind

with a drowsy desire,

my limbs heavy

with want,

my body

ripe with need;

he is the master

of seduction,

beginning with

my brain.

I wish I could tell you

exactly what

you mean to me

but I cannot

find the words,

for you leave me

speechless

every single time.

Your tongue,

it wraps around mine

so possessively,

teasing me in firm strokes,

bringing me to rapture

as I savour you

so completely –

and when you move it lower,

I'm in heaven.

I want you to

carve your love

into my willing flesh

until I scream,

thrusting deep within

to the very heart of me,

owning me

with no mercy.

And, then…

Her

Good Girl

She dresses carefully to meet him, the outfit
he had chosen laid out piece-by-piece on the
bed. Gossamer-thin stockings, smooth and
soft as they slide over her skin; panties, a
mere scrap of lace. Matching bra, balconette
with a strip of lace across the top, and straps
that criss-cross over her chest, pushing up her
breast so they jut before her, eagerly awaiting
his touch. His favourite suspender belt and
LBD, slim-fitting and hip-skimming,
covering her body yet leaving little to the
imagination. His collar at her throat, snug
and familiar.

Her long brunette hair is pulled back and up
into a tight ponytail, high on her head and
spilling down her back. He loves her hair
long and loose, flowing around her face, yet
on occasions like these, his request is that it is
tied back. Out of the way. Easier for him to
grasp and pull.

At the thought of this, she shivers and the sweet, secret place between her legs tightens, then loosens, leaving her panties damp. She feels weak with desire, heady with lust. Her body quivers ever so slightly in anticipation, yet her limbs are languid.

She takes a sip of white wine, relishing the cool, crisp taste in her mouth. Just a taster; no more until he allows it. He doesn't want her drunk at the beginning of their encounter. He wants her collected, in control, until he says otherwise. He wants to be the one who loosens her inhibitions, who musses her hair, who causes her to forget her name and cry out his.

She checks the time on the digital clock on the nightstand. Four minutes and he will arrive; always prompt, never keeping her waiting. She smoothes the bedclothes, checks her reflection in the mirrored wardrobe, tucks a stray lock of hair behind her ear. Her insides fizz, swoon, tighten. Her breath catches in her throat as she hears the ping of the elevator doors in the corridor.

He is here.

A pause, a beat, a quiet movement outside the door, and then a knock on the panelled wood.

She moves to the door, her steps elegant and measured in her heels, controlling the impulse to rush. She swings the door open and he is there. Tall, dark hair curling at the nape of his neck, tailored suit smart and unruffled, blue eyes on her.

She smiles and moves back to allow him entry.

"Good evening, Sir." Her voice is husky and low.

In one smooth move, he kicks the door shut behind him and reaches for her, drawing her into his arms. In a rare moment of uncontrolled passion, he takes her face between his hands and kisses her, deeply and ardently, working her lips with his own, darting his tongue into her mouth and ravishing her. She begins to kiss him back, but he suddenly stops, pushes her back, holding her arms close to her sides, his eyes heavy-lidded and caressing.

"Assume your position, kitten," he says, his voice deep, throaty, yet firm.

As she instinctively falls into the Nadu pose, she knows that the night is going to be intensely pleasurable for them both.

She is an alluring mix

of wild desire,

tempestuous

passion,

and gently,

steady devotion,

and it is a combination that

he finds impossible

to resist.

She is wild

and wanton

and her heart

will dive right in,

or not at all,

for you must tempt her

with the strength

of your loyalty

and a connection

that is pure,

or you won't

catch her at all.

She isn't looking

for a prince;

she is waiting for

a scarred and weary warrior,

searching for a place

to call home,

yet ready to head

into battle for her and

their love.

She doesn't want

soft and gentle;

she wants

rough and passionate,

loving to the point

of madness,

and it has to be

soul-deep.

She is used to starting over. And she will do it again and again until she finds the one who sets her soul alight, makes her heart skip a beat, and cradles her emotions in his hands with a gentleness that makes her swoon.

One day, she will find him…

Her heart is

a wild animal,

just waiting for

someone to call home,

while his is

steady and sure,

longing for a soulmate

to run free with –

they are a perfect match.

My breath is hitched

as a shiver

runs across my body;

goosebumps raise my skin

in delicate patterns,

desire dripping from me

in a torrent of passion –

you do this to me;

only you.

It starts in my mind,

that slow seduction,

tantalising

my thoughts,

teasing my fantasies,

making me

feel safe enough

to share my

deepest desires –

just knowing that

this is exclusive,

committed,

open and honest

is the biggest

aphrodisiac ever.

She is a one-man woman. And, in a world
full of players, and cheats, and the
polyamorous, she will wait patiently for her
one-woman man.

Write her a melody

dressed in shades of passion,

and honesty,

and commitment,

and love;

draw it on her soul in

indelible ink

and watch her blossom in

all the right ways.

She wants real love,

honest, loyal,

and raw,

never mediocre

or half-hearted;

explorations of

mind, body,

and soul,

deep conversations

that move her,

commitment and

affection,

sensuality and

passion;

she offers

all of this and more

and will not accept

anything less.

There is nothing casual about her. She wants to know everything about you, from your favourite childhood memory to the sounds that you make when she shows you the depth of her love.

Her sighs

speak a language

that only he

understands,

and he loves

to hear her

utter them,

over and over again.

Her body

will only truly

come alive

for the one who

deserves it,

and she will know

who you are;

true nakedness

and desire

only arrives when

you look beyond the form

and embrace the soul.

She isn't naked

until you have

undressed every aspect

of her soul

and caressed her heart

with hands that are

gentle yet rough

in all the

right moments.

There is a freak

hidden

just below

the surface,

waiting for the

right man

to coax

her out.

She doesn't need roses, or diamonds, or designer clothing. She just needs him and the knowledge that he is committed to their love with every ounce of his being.

Her love is private,

exclusive,

and committed,

and if you can

show her

the same in return,

she will drop

her guard

and open up for you

in ways you

have only ever

dreamt of;

cherish her heart

and set her body alight

for only you.

I don't want hesitation,

I don't want

second thoughts,

I don't want decisions

and comparisons

to someone else;

either you choose me

with no reason to stall,

or you walk away.

I crave passion

like my body

craves air,

I need emotion

or I cannot truly feel you,

I want intimacy

to draw us

all the more closer,

and if we have

all of that,

then love won't be

far behind.

She just wants someone who will look past the exterior to see the real woman within, and who will love and accept every quirk, flaw, and imperfection, simply because they are hers.

Can you see me

beneath these silken wrappers

and the eyeliner flick?

It is my armour,

but look past that,

or close your eyes

and feel me;

without devouring what I am,

try to glimpse who I am.

She has a heart

that is gentle

but that loves

like a storm;

never underestimate

her capacity

for passion.

I don't want

just hand-holding and

forehead kisses;

I want hair pulling,

I want passion,

I want you to push me

against the wall

and devour me with your lips –

I want you to fuck me

until I can't

remember my name.

I want it all.

There is nothing

that turns her on more

than respect,

understanding, passion,

and commitment,

so meet her halfway,

show her that

you want her,

and don't waste her time.

There are days when

she needs

to be loved, and

there are days

when she needs

 to be taken,

roughly;

there are days when

she needs both,

yet she knows that

you can satisfy her

in all the right ways.

And, then…

Them

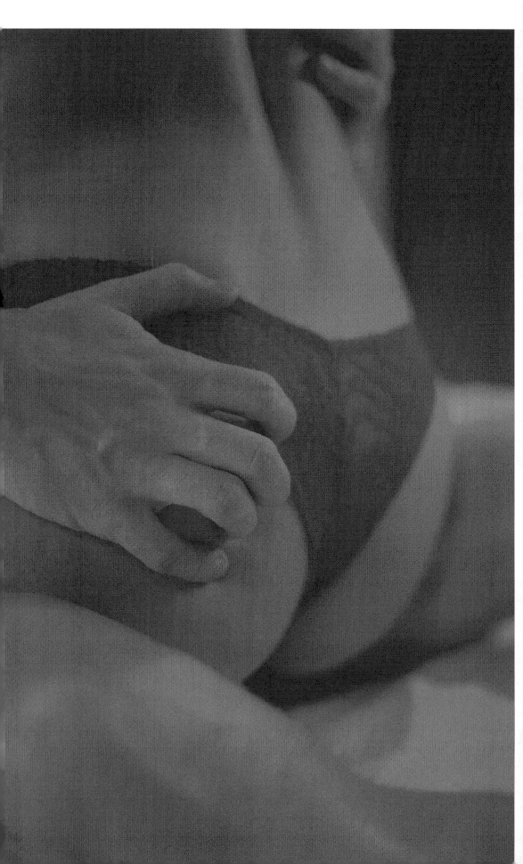

Make love to me;

I want to feel

your weight

on top of me,

and your hands

on my wrists,

and your voice

in my ear,

as you take me

mercilessly,

our sweat mingling,

my skin tingling,

as we move in unison

to the beat

of our love.

I want your fears, your joy, your scars, and your sadness. I want the way you look in the morning, and the way you hold my hand. I want your thoughts, your frustrations, and the words you leave unsaid. I want all of your flaws and imperfections. I want you.

She has never felt

a love like this

before,

a craving

of such intensity

that he is on her mind

all of the time;

she wants to lose herself in

her delicious fantasy.

Come to me,

let me show you

this secret

world within me,

where only

the two of us

will exist,

in a tangle of dreams,

and bodies, and desires.

I love nothing more

than to

lose myself in you

and this intense,

burning desire

between us;

you ignite a fire in me

that is hard

to contain.

You. You make all of my days worthwhile.
You fill my heart with love like I've never
known before. You are the reason my life
feels so suddenly and unexpectedly complete.
You.

I want to

undress for you,

and not just my body –

I want to shed

everything;

these self-erected walls,

my fears and

inhibitions,

the reasons I hide

my heart –

I want to lay myself

bare to you.

Come closer,

place your hands

over me

and on me,

feel the truth

in my heart –

this body

won't ever lie.

Your hands

trace a journey

of such

exquisite pleasure

that my body

shivers

under your touch

and my heart swells

with love for you.

He dominates my dreams and runs riot
through my imagination. When we are
together, a fire ignites between us that burns
within me while we are apart. He is my all-
consuming passion, and I am his.

I will worship you

as you

worship me,

wildly,

passionately,

yet with the

utmost respect;

with reverence,

I submit to you

completely

with every fibre

of my being –

I am yours.

The chemistry

between us

is profound,

undeniably erotic

and as explosive

as a thunderstorm;

when you touch me,

my desire

ignites like

a lightning bolt,

strong enough

to set the

both of us alight

with the flame

of passion.

The connection

between us

is pure magic

and you are

the magician

with skilled hands,

a sensual tongue,

and the

ability to weave

a spell of

pure enchantment

over my body

and my mind.

Our love will never be perfect. But it is loyal, and fun, and serious, and messy, and, above all else, *healthy*. And that is perfect for me.

I cannot deny

the way your love

consumes me

and this mad,

reckless passion

between us

drives me wild

with wanton desire;

you are my everything.

You leave me

in pieces;

melting,

exquisite pieces;

whenever you

touch me,

your hands

tantalisingly

strong and sure,

yet irresistibly

erotic,

taking control

of my body,

and firing up

my soul.

I love the way

your body

fits so neatly

against my curves,

and your soul

merges

so beautifully

with mine.

It is the type of love that I never knew existed, yet dreamed of anyway. I can be myself with him; my crazy, impatient, occasionally unreasonable, loving and loyal self with him, and he embraces it all and worships the ground I walk on. I need never doubt him. This is it. This is real love.

You are everything

I have been

waiting for

yet nothing

I have

encountered

before;

trust, empathy,

and forever.

I never expected

to fall for you

so quickly

and so

completely,

but the way

you caught me –

so firmly,

and passionately,

yet with a

gentleness

that can't be compared –

meant that I

was utterly ensnared,

utterly yours.

I want to

slow down time

and spend

forever

in this moment

with you

as our limbs

entwine

and our hearts beat as one.

Your touch

leaves a silken trail

of molten desire

gliding down

my body,

setting my nerves

on fire until

we both ignite

with the strength of our passion.

Caught on a knife-edge

between passion

and pain,

I am lost

in a world of

bottomless desire;

you have me

begging,

begging you for more.

He is like a drug to me; my sweetest obsession, my deepest, darkest desire. My love for him is passion, contentment, and starry-eyed delight, for he matches my feelings and is not afraid to show it.

I want to

wrap myself

around you

and envelop you

in the warmth of me;

these arms

tightly wound

across your back,

these legs

gripping your hips –

every part of me

welcomes you within.

Take me

passionately

and with

fevered urgency;

I want to feel

your teeth

on my neck

and your hands

on my wrists

and the weight of

your body

on mine,

holding me down,

keeping me

anchored.

I love it when

you make a

beautiful mess of me,

hair tousled,

skin flushed,

eyes drowsy,

and breath jagged;

can you see

what you do to me?

Only love and

mutual trust

can get me there.

You see the beast

in me, and

you embrace it

thoroughly,

coaxing it out,

caressing its flaws,

holding it close

so you can experience

every bump in

the road;

our demons

always play well together.

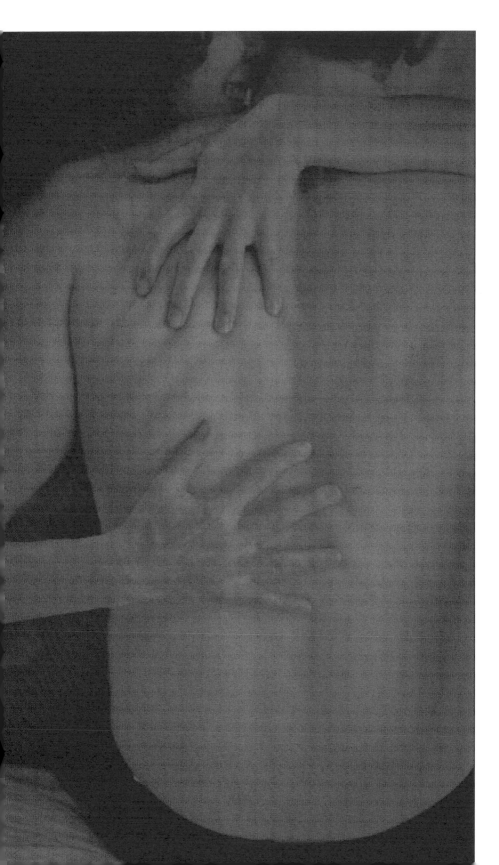

And it wasn't his looks, or his job, or his money that kept her, but the fact that he could hear the things she didn't say.

My thoughts

are sinful

when they come

to you,

and we could

ignite a flame

with the intensity

of this spark

between us;

a steady burn

that need never

extinguish.

I don't want perfect love;

I want love that

bites and scratches

but doesn't bruise;

love that

pulls and grasps

yet never turns away;

love that is

passionate and

tempestuous

but that never gives up;

a warrior's love,

scarred and

imperfect, yet

loyal and brave.

I want to fill myself

to the brim

with every part of you,

I want soft yet

greedy kisses,

I want hands in

my hair,

I want your thoughts

and your feelings,

I want those

secret sounds that you make

just for me;

I want all of you,

on me and in me and

all around me.

We have no need

for words

when we can

communicate

with our bodies,

and this desire

for each other,

hot and demanding

yet so, so sweet,

and the way

your soul

speaks to mine

on so many

different levels

is more than enough.

I am a mess

of tight peaks

and slippery troughs,

my body responding

most admirably to you,

as your gaze

caresses my nakedness,

so hot, it almost

feels like touch,

running down my torso,

lingering

in the places

I want you the most;

take me,

make me come undone.

There is a storm

building within me,

between my thighs,

and its your touch

that incites it,

you are taking me high.

Your tongue feels like heaven,

tracing up and down,

my pleasure increases,

my lust knows no bounds.

You spread me so wide

to concentrate on that spot,

and I just cannot help it,

my body is so hot.

I begin to moan loudly,

and clutch at your hair,

pulling you closer;

oh, please – right there!

Don't stop, don't stop –

and you carry on

as I shatter completely,

my passion come completely

undone.

She says,

move closer

so I can feel your soul

against mine,

and you can sink into me

as you find a home

within these curves,

fitting neatly

into the space

that I have reserved

for you;

my twin flame –

my soulmate.

I wrap myself

around you

 as we merge

our bodies

into one,

and you move me

like nobody

has done before;

I can feel you

deep inside me,

caressing my heart,

caressing my soul.

There is nothing

quite like

the way I can

open myself

to you fully,

safe in the knowledge

that you will accept

every part of me,

caressing my flaws

as confidently as

you caress my curves.

Touch me here,

kiss me there,

feel my heartbeat

under your hand;

it beats

a tattoo for you,

the drums of

forever love,

so sink into me

and let us

dance to the rhythm

together.

Bondage-tied –

against these ropes, I writhe,

waiting for your touch,

arms and legs

spread wide.

My body is slick,

juices overflow,

and your voice washes

over me,

seductive and slow.

But I need more than this,

as your words tantalise,

I need you inside me,

feeling you slide

right into my depths,

beginning to pound,

gripping my hips,

while I'm still bound.

I want to feel used,

and sated within,

my body parts tingling,

overtaken by sin.

But you know what you're doing,

this isn't the first,

and keeping me waiting

increases your thirst.

When you finally take me,

my ability to speak

will have fled these bones

as my intense passion peaks.

All I can do is scream,

and moan and cry out;

this is what you crave,

when this love-lust between us

is never in doubt.

Bodies bared

and sensually entwined

as you move

above me

and I cling on

for dear life

as you take me

to places

I have never been

before,

exquisitely intimate,

beautifully lustful,

filled with

passion,

bonded by love.

Passion speaks

in silent words

and decisive actions,

hands that take

yet give so much

pleasure,

lips always ready

to kiss,

to tease,

to tantalise,

tracing trails of

delicious desire

that pools

in the pit of my stomach,

leaving me

wet and wanton.

Your eager kisses

sweep me away

on an ocean

of desire;

your love

is my lifeboat,

my saviour,

the passion that

sets me adrift,

and the

sanctuary that

brings me back

to dry land –

immerse me in

your sea of devotion.

Enter me,

slide inside my soul

as you slide

inside my body,

caressing all of me

as you sink within;

savour

the essence of me

right from

my heart,

and I will hold

you close,

welcoming you

as you reach

my very core.

She has a wild side

a headstrong nature,

but he has

the power to tame her,

to harness the wild streak,

and to hold her tight,

close to his heart,

until she surrenders

to him, and the raw desire.

Kiss me

with lips as dark

as poison

and eyes as

black as sin.

I imagine you,

dreams so vivid,

so real,

intoxicating my mind,

infusing my body

with dark desire.

I need you to

pull me closer,

as close as you can,

so there is no

space between us,

and we move as one;

skin on skin, heart on heart,

so close

our souls are connected.

I dream of a time

when there is

no space

between us,

and I can taste

the words left unsaid

on the caress

of your breath.

Deliciously dark,

sensual fantasies

segue into sinful delights;

you make every time

seem like the best,

and, as I succumb

to this raw desire,

I offer myself

to you, for all time.

Sometimes,

I think he knows

my body

better than I

know myself,

strumming me

like a bass guitar,

making me

writhe and hum.

He made love to her

with such passion

that the memory of him

was imprinted

on her soul

for days afterwards.

Your skin

against mine

is the only real

I want to feel;

your mouth on my lips,

your hands on my hips,

and when you

finally take me,

I am most assuredly all yours.

Afterword

I would just like to thank everyone who has purchased my book. I appreciate it so much. I hope you enjoyed my poetry and prose, and that you found something within my musings that you could relate to.

For more poetry, you can find me on Instagram at @herundiscloseddesires. I would love for you to join me there.

Alternatively, look for me at @fragmentspoetry.

Photo credits:

Pg. 6 - Omid Armin via Unsplash.com

Pg. 16 – James Barr via Unsplash.com

Pg. 60 – christian buehner via Unsplash.com

Pg. 94 - Malik Skydsgaard via Unsplash.com

Pg. 120 – Gabe Rebra via Unsplash.com

Pg. 137 – Artem Labunsky via Unsplash.com

Pg. 141, 184, 224 – Dainis Graveris via Unsplash.com